the 4 CHAIRS

the 4 CHAIRS

Discovering what your spiritual life looks like from God's point of view

ADRIAN DESPRES

KBM MEDIA
Hearts on fire, lives on purpose

The 4 Chairs
Adrian Despres
ISBN No. 978-0-9819403-0-4
©2008 by Adrian Despres. All rights reserved.

Published by KBM Media, a division of Kingdom Building Ministries,
14485 E. Evans Ave., Aurora, Colorado 80014.

Visit us online at www.kbm.org.
For more about Adrian Despres, visit www.adriandespres.com.

Dedication

Dedicated to my wife, Lisa—my blonde-haired, blue-eyed, righteous fox. I truly appreciate everything that you do for the Kingdom, and I love you.

Acknowledgements

I would like to thank several people for helping me with this project. First, thank you to my wife, Lisa, and my four children: Rachel, Branson, Kaitlyn, and Benjamin. You're an awesome family.

This has been a team project. Thank you to Mark Vermilion for helping me organize, edit, and wordsmith this book. And thank you to April Epperson for taking my spoken messages (with all my crazy tangents) and first capturing them in writing.

I want to be like you guys when I grow up.

Contents

Introduction

HAVE A SEAT

IMAGINE FOUR CHAIRS sitting side by side on a stage in an auditorium filled with people. The room is pretty dark except for where the chairs are sitting. They're lit up by several spotlights. It doesn't really matter what the chairs look like. They could be metal folding chairs (my preference), or they could be plush, overstuffed chairs—the kind you'd have in your family room.

There's really only one thing that matters about these chairs. It's the fact that you're sitting in one of them. *Which one are you sitting in?*

The Chair You Choose
These chairs aren't just any ordinary chairs. They represent the spiritual places where you and I (and everyone in the world) can sit. Each of us is sitting in one of them.

The first chair is the one God desires for us to sit in. The second chair is the one I believe most Christians are sitting in. The third chair is the most dangerous one because it's hard to know if you're really in it or not (I'll explain that later). And the fourth chair is the one that most of the world's population—including most of your neighbors and co-workers—are sitting in.

We all sit in one of these chairs whether we want to or not.

The good news is, you get to choose which chair you're in. In fact, it's the most important choice you'll make in your whole life. Why? Because the chair you choose will determine how you live this life and where you'll spend all of eternity.

Keep this picture of the four chairs in mind. In the pages ahead, I'll help you more fully understand the spiritual condition that each represents. I'll ask you to consider which chair you're sitting in. And you can be sure of one more thing: If you're not in the first chair, I'll ask you to trade places and get there as quickly as possible.

So, have a seat. It won't take you long to read this book, but the next few moments may change your life forever.

Chapter 1

THE FIRST CHAIR // Crazy

I'M MADLY IN LOVE WITH MY WIFE, LISA. I have been since shortly after we met in college.

I was majoring in biology, and she was studying chemistry. We had only been dating a few months when I realized I was crazy about her. So, I made a plan to show her how much I cared.

I bought her a dozen "college roses" (otherwise known as carnations) and waited for her outside of her chemistry lab. I found a prime location in the middle of the hallway, got down on my knees, and held the carnations to my chest. I cleared my throat and waited.

The lab door opened and people started filling the hallway. As soon as I saw her blonde head bobbing toward me, I started singing Joe Cocker's song, "You Are So Beautiful."

I sang really loud.

"You are so beautiful to me. Can't you see? You're everything I've hoped for. You're everything I need…"

People stopped and stared at me. Then they started trying to figure out who I was singing to. I could hear people whispering, "Is he singing to you?" and others answering, "No way, not me!"

When Lisa saw me, she froze. Her face turned bright red. It didn't take long before everyone knew who I was singing to. And, I'm telling you, the crowd in between us parted like the Red Sea.

Of course, the response from all the women was, "Awww!" All the guys just gritted their teeth and said, "Shut up, man, you're making us look bad!"

I didn't care if I looked stupid. I wanted Lisa to know how I felt.

People do crazy things when they're in love.

The Things We Do For Love

You can usually tell when people are deeply in love. They act differently than everyone else. They do crazy things.

Weird things.

Extreme things.

They're not ashamed to show the one they love how much they care.

My friend Dwight Robertson says it this way: "We'll do things for love that we won't do for any other reason."

I'll give you an example. I played football in college. My roommate and I were slobs. I mean we were disgusting. People used to take pictures of our dorm room and send them home to their moms with a note that said, "See mom, I'm not the messiest person in the world!"

Every day after practice or class, we came in and dropped our clothes on the floor. It was an act of worship, of course, because God created gravity. If we put our clothes away, we would be working against God. So, we did what we could to honor the Lord. (Yeah, right. Whatever.)

I'll give you a couple of examples of how disgusting we were. One day, a young lady asked my roommate and me if we could fix her

bicycle. We puffed out our chests and said, "Sure, of course we can fix it."

We took the bike back to our room and fixed it in about five minutes. The only thing wrong with it was that the chain had fallen off. (It was so easy that we took the chain off and started racing to see who could put it back on the fastest. Thirty-eight seconds was the record, I think.)

The only problem was, we didn't tell her it was fixed.

Seven weeks later, she knocked on our door and asked if her bike was ready. I looked at my roommate and whispered, "I thought you gave it back to her." He said, "No, I thought you did." We both looked at her and said, "Somebody must have stolen your bike!"

My roommate had a hunch that the bike was still somewhere in our room. We started digging through the mess and, sure enough, her bicycle was buried under all of our sweaty clothes. Can you believe that? We were so disgusting that we actually lost a ten-speed bicycle in our dorm room!

If you're still not convinced I was a slob, let me share a few more disgusting things that happened my freshmen year in college. Somebody once made my roommate some stew. (The key to a football player's heart is through his stomach.) It was so good that we decided not to throw away what we didn't eat. I put the lid back on the plastic storage container it came in and placed it next to my bed.

Somehow, during the course of the next few days, the container got shoved under my bed. I forgot about it.

People would come into our room and ask, "What's that smell?" My roommate and I would say, "What smell?"

That was in the fall.

When we got ready to move home for the summer, it was my job to clean out under the beds. After about three hours, I found the container. I thought, "Food!" I took off the lid, and there were plants growing and bugs crawling around in it!

But those weren't the only bugs crawling around in our room. We also had cockroaches. (Maybe the stew had something to do with the cockroaches!) We had posters on our walls, and when we flicked the middle of the posters, it was so cool because we got a symmetrical response—roaches darting out in every direction.

When I got to my mom's house for summer break, she was standing in the front yard, waiting for me. I opened the door to get out of the car and give her a big hug, and she yelled, "Stay in the car! I want to set off a roach bomb before you bring anything into this house." It took about ten minutes, but I finally convinced her to first let me out of the car.

So what does all of this have to do with being crazy in love? Well, I'm getting to that. You see, my wife is the exact opposite of me. I'm a slob, and she's a clean freak. She's so clean that I'm convinced she can stand in the kitchen and hear a piece of dirt hit the floor in the living room.

Let me give you a picture of how different she is than me. One evening, a hurricane was pounding South Carolina, the state where we live. Lisa was vacuuming the floor when the winds knocked out our electricity. I went upstairs and rounded up our kids to make sure they were okay. When I returned downstairs, I couldn't see anything, but I could hear a swish-swish sound.

"Lisa, what are you doing?" I asked.

"What do you think I'm doing? I'm sweeping the floor!" she fired back.

"But it's completely dark. How can you sweep in the dark?"

"I don't need any light," she replied confidently. "I know exactly where every piece of dirt is in my house!"

That's how clean she is.

Needless to say, when I married Lisa after college, I knew I'd have to change. Actually, I wanted to change because I loved her so much. I wanted her to know how much I loved her with every little thing I did.

The day we came home from our honeymoon, I emptied my sock drawer (the one full of unmatched socks that was passed down from my grandfather to my dad to me). That day, I sat on the floor and matched socks for two hours.

I don't know why socks have to match anyway. Nobody sees them. But it matters to my wife, so I matched socks. I didn't want to wake up Lisa in the morning by turning on the lights to find matching socks. So, I lined up my socks in the drawer by color: blue on the left, black on the right, and all the other colors in the middle (because blue and black can get mixed up in the dark).

I've been married for more than twenty years, and my socks are still in order.

But that's not all I do because I love her. I also rinse the dishes before I put them in the dishwasher. I'll never understand why dishes need to be rinsed first. Isn't that what the dishwasher is supposed to do? But my wife likes it when I rinse the dishes before I put them into the dishwasher. So, I do.

But I do more than just arrange my socks and rinse the dishes. I also fluff and arrange the decorative pillows on our bed. I'll never know why we need decorative pillows. What purpose do they serve? I'm not even allowed to put my head on them! But my wife likes decorative pillows, so I make the bed every day and fluff and neatly arrange the pillows. Sometimes, I even get creative and spell out things or make shapes like a heart or a cross.

Pairing socks so they match. Rinsing the dishes before I put them in the dishwasher. Fluffing and arranging the decorative pillows. Those aren't the kinds of things a slob does. But my wife feels loved when I do things around the house that are important to her. So, I do them.

Like I said, *people do crazy things when they're in love.*

Going To Extremes

I've just given you a picture of Christians who are sitting in the first chair. They're crazy in love with Jesus. They go to extremes to show Him how much they love Him. And they're willing to change anything and everything to please Him.

I think the psalmist David understood this kind of crazy love. He was so in love with God that he danced around the streets without any clothes on! And when his wife questioned him about his behavior, he said, "I'll become even more undignified than this!" (2 Samuel 6:22).

Now, I'm not suggesting that you *totally* follow David's example. (For one thing, it's against the law to run around the streets naked.) But are you willing to go to extremes to express your love for God? Or are you too concerned about what other people think to show that you're crazy in love with Him?

First-chair Christians have a love for Jesus that shows in all areas of their lives.

For one thing, it shows in the way they obey God. They may not understand everything He asks of them, but they willingly obey. Not begrudgingly, but joyfully—as an expression of their love for Him.

Jesus made it clear that love and obedience go hand in hand. He once said, "If you love me, you **will** obey my commands" (John 14:15, emphasis mine). Don't misunderstand the meaning of this. The key is not obedience. It's love. If you have trouble with obedience, it's not because you need more discipline. You need more love.

First-chair Christians also want to know Him better. That's why they study the Bible and pray. Not because they have to, but because they want to. They want to know Him better, and they've learned that you have to spend time with Him and listen to what He says through His Word in order to know Him.

What if Lisa and I stopped spending time together after we got married? How strong would our relationship be two months later? Two years later? Twenty years later? It's no different in our relationship with God. If we don't spend time with Him, our relationship grows cold.

First-chair Christians also know that God's Word provides guidance for their life (Psalm 119:105) and protection from sin (Psalm 119:9).

First-chair Christians express their love for God in other ways as well. For one thing, they talk about Him—a lot. It comes natural. They're like a guy talking about his girlfriend, or a girl talking about her boyfriend. They can't help themselves. They want to tell everyone how great their girlfriend or boyfriend is. Do you talk that way about God?

Likewise, first-chair Christians want everyone to meet God. They know He's the greatest thing in the universe, and they want everyone else to know Him, too. They're constantly introducing people to Him. Why wouldn't they?

Each of these things increasingly grows in the lives of first-chair Christians. But don't get me wrong. You don't measure life in the first chair with a performance-based approval rating. The key isn't your performance—how much Bible you read, how much time you spend in prayer, or how many people you introduce to Christ. The key is that your love for God and people motivates you to grow in each of these areas.

It's what my businessman friend Tobin Cassels calls CMI, which is short for *Continuous Measurable Improvement*. We want to be closer to God this week, this month, this year than we were last week, last month, last year.

People in the first chair may be spiritual babes or spiritual sages. What they have in common is that they love God with all their heart, soul, mind, and strength. And their crazy love for God spills over into a crazy love for people.

Louder Than Words

The woman who anointed Jesus' feet in Luke chapter seven truly loved Jesus. We don't just know it because Luke said it. We know it because of what she did.

In Jesus' day, a dinner would often take place outside, in plain view of the neighbors. The people who weren't invited could see what was going on, but they also knew the party was only for those invited. There was no wall or fence keeping them from the party, but there was an invisible line they knew they shouldn't cross.

This woman, however, stepped over that line and made her way to Jesus.

She was carrying a box of expensive perfume called alabaster that would've cost her a year's worth of wages. It was probably the most valuable thing she owned.

One of the Pharisees told Jesus she was "a sinner." More than likely, this meant she was a prostitute. She probably earned the money she used to buy the perfume by selling her body.

When she laid the perfume before the Lord, it was like she was laying her sinful lifestyle at His feet. Then she worshipped Jesus.

She wet His feet with her tears. She wiped them with her hair. She kissed them and anointed them with her perfume.

Simon said to himself, "If this man were a prophet, he would know who is touching him and what kind of woman she is—that she is a sinner." Notice, Simon only said this to himself, but Jesus answered him anyway.

Jesus reminded Simon that he had not given Jesus any water to wash His feet—as was customary in their day. On the other hand, the sinful woman did more than give Jesus water to wash His feet. She had anointed His feet with expensive perfume.

Jesus said, "Therefore I tell you, her sins, which are many, are forgiven—for she **loved much**. But he who has been forgiven little, loves little" (Luke 7:47, emphasis mine).

This woman loved Jesus so much that she went to extremes to show it. She didn't just give Him what was customary in her day. She was extravagant in her offering—giving Jesus her most costly possession.

This story clearly shows us what it means to be a first-chair Christian. It means loving God with more than words. It means loving Him in extreme—and possibly weird and crazy—ways.

People do crazy things when they're in love.

What crazy thing have you done for God lately?

Chapter 2

THE SECOND CHAIR // Lukewarm

LISA AND I HAVE BEEN MARRIED FOR TWENTY YEARS. You already know I'm crazy about her. But over time, I've noticed that some things have changed in our relationship. I don't always treat her the same as I did when we first got married—especially if there's a good football game on TV.

On game day a few years ago, I was lying on the couch with my feet propped up on the arm (my six-foot-six body won't fully fit on the couch), and I was making slob noises like "Hugh, Argh, Ahugh."

It's a man thing.

Then, I caught myself saying something to Lisa that's really bad: "Lisa, when you finish carrying the laundry basket upstairs, would you get me something to drink?"

Time out: I'm sorry, but that request is straight from the pit of Hell. It's amazing to me that we men will often treat our secretaries better than our wives. If a secretary is carrying something heavy, we offer to help. Why don't we do the same with our wives?

Now, here's the deal: I never used to make those guttural noises around Lisa when we were dating. Instead, I'd say strange (but loving) things like "Shnookem, shnoopsy, pookie bear."

And I never used to treat her like a waitress. Back then, I was always looking for *what I could do for her.*

My brains must have fallen out somewhere in the years since we were married. (Maybe it's because of all those hits to the head I took in football.) But something changed. What was it?

The Bible clearly says that I'm supposed to love my wife as much as Christ loves the church and gave Himself up for her. Translation: I'm supposed to love my wife as much as Jesus loved me when He was brutally killed on the cross in my place!

And here I am ordering my wife around as if she's my slave. When I do that, it's a sign that I've gotten used to her. I'm taking her for granted.

And it's not right.

She's still the off-the-heazy, righteous fox that God gave to be my wife—for me to love and cherish. Why do I get used to her and take her for granted? Why is it sometimes easier for me to treat perfect strangers better than I treat my best friend?

Maybe you aren't married and can't exactly relate, but I'm sure you know what I'm talking about. You've probably done the same thing with your parents, siblings, or close friends. I spend time with kids all over the nation as I speak at youth events, and one of the most common things I see is that they don't treat their parents with love and respect.

Over the course of time, it's easy for all of us—husbands, wives, and children—to get used to each other and take each other for granted. It's human nature. But it's also very, very wrong.

Husbands, I can tell what you think about Jesus by how lovingly you treat your wife. Wives, I can tell what you think about God by how well you submit to your husband. And children, I can tell how much respect you have for God by the way you respect your parents.

Getting Used to God

We don't just take people for granted. We take God for granted, too. We start out excited about Him. We live to serve Him. But as the months and years go by, our love for Him grows cold. We stop searching the depths of God's love. We somehow imagine Him as less than He is, and we believe the lie that it's no big deal to know Him.

But let me correct that lie: It's a very big deal! And He's a very big God worth every ounce of love and respect we give Him! There are no words to describe how great He is!

In fact, John Wesley once wrote a hymn that said, "O for a thousand tongues to sing my great Redeemer's praise." He recognized that words can't describe how great God is.

But, as we walk with him month after month, we begin to lose sight of His greatness. And before long, we treat Him like He's ordinary… or worse.

I've just described what happens with people who are sitting in the second chair. They're Christians who've been around the church for so long that God is not as important to them as He should be. They sing songs and listen to sermons about Jesus, but sadly, they've lost their love for Him.

Over time, passion fades and love grows cold.

Have I just described you? Is this the chair you're sitting in?

My First Day in Church

I became a Christian during two-a-day football practices before my freshman year in college. I stumbled into my dorm room the very first night—after I had gone out drinking—and my roommate, Mark Cagle, met me at the door. He gave me a big hug and said, "How's it going?" I jumped up on my bunk bed and looked down at him sitting at his desk.

"What are you reading?" I asked.

He looked up at me and smiled. "I'm reading the Bible!"

God used that simple encounter to change my life. As I lied there in bed, my eyes began to well up with tears. God began to convict me that my sin hurt Him. I confessed thirty-one sins that night. I said to Him, "God, if there's a truck coming down the street, and someone is about to get hit by it, I'll push them out of the way and die for them—because I now know you."

The next morning, I got up early and read the whole book of Matthew. I couldn't put it down. By the end of the week, I'd read the whole New Testament.

The following Sunday, I got up early to go to church—I was so excited. I decided to get some of my other football buddies to go with me. I went from room to room and shouted, "Hey guys, get up. We're going to church!"

But Sunday was our one day of the week to sleep in, and my teammates weren't pleased that I was waking them up so early.

"Shut up, man!" they shouted back. "We're not getting up! We're sleeping!"

I replied, "You shut up! You're going to church!" (See, I didn't know you aren't supposed to say "shut up." Now, I say, "hush.")

Finally, some of them realized I wasn't going to give up, so they decided to get up and go with me.

Imagine the picture: I crammed eight huge football players wearing leisure suits into my custom Nova sweet ride. No, I'm just kidding. I was actually the only guy wearing a leisure suit, but most of them *were* wearing sock ties. As we drove to church, they were all thinking about the nap they were going to take when we got back. I was thinking about where we were going to sit.

See, if I go to a basketball or football game, I want to sit as close to the action as possible. So, I'm thinking the same thing about going to church: I want to be as close to the front as possible. I'm thinking

that would put me as close to God as possible. But I figured you'd have to get there earlier than everyone else to get a front-row seat. I didn't know that people at most churches don't sit in the front. I didn't know they arrive early to get back-row seats.

Of course, we were ten minutes late. (We were five minutes late because we were college students and another five minutes late because we were football players.) I walked in the back of the sanctuary and spotted an empty row in the front. I couldn't believe it. A front-row seat!

My buddies who'd grown up in church stopped in the back and saw me headed for the front row. They tried to stop me.

"No! Adrian, not the first row! Stop!"

But it was too late. My radar was locked on the front row like a search-and-destroy missile. There was no stopping me.

I walked quickly down to the front row and plopped down. My buddies straggled reluctantly behind and sat down next to me. You should've seen me. I sat with my legs stretched out in front of me. My arms were stretched out each direction down the back of the pew—around several of my buddies' shoulders. I didn't have any etiquette. I didn't know how you're expected to act in church.

But I was about to find out.

We started singing some songs. At first, I didn't care for the tune, but the words were pretty cool. Then, this guy started preaching. Now, remember, I had just read the whole New Testament, and the preacher was giving a message from the New Testament. I had just read the passage he was preaching on! And the preacher was helping me understand what it meant.

I couldn't stop taking notes. It was awesome!

I probably shouldn't have turned around and looked behind me. That was when I was introduced to second-chair Christians.

I saw two evil things behind me. Evil thing number one: I saw people dozing off. I thought, "What in the world? People are sleeping when the preacher is talking about God? Why aren't they excited?"

And then I saw evil thing number two: I saw people looking at their watches. I got distracted for a moment as I saw one guy try to hide what he was doing by scratching his elbow on his wrist as he glanced at his watch. Then I saw another guy turn and pretend to stretch his arm and neck as he strained to see the clock on the back wall. (C'mon, nobody stretches like that in real life!)

I started crying.

I thought, "Why don't these people love God? Why don't they want to worship Him and learn more about Him?"

That was my first exposure to second-chair Christianity. And I've seen a lot of it since. In fact, I've found that it rules most churches.

Over time, passion fades and love grows cold.

Uncomfortable

Second-chair people think that first-chair people are radical and even fanatical, and they say, "Hey, would you settle down? You're turning people off!"

They don't realize that, according to the Bible, first-chair people are not fanatical at all. They're normal.

Have you ever been around someone who's totally in love with God, and it makes you feel uncomfortable? You know why it makes you feel that way? It's because those people make you aware of your own apathy. Second-chair Christians try to douse first-chair Christians with the cold water of criticism to get them to cool down their passion for God. They want first-chair Christians to join them in the second chair so they can feel better about their own apathy. It's awful, but it's happening all around us in the church.

Now, what I'm about to say is controversial—it may even cause you to put down this book—but I'm convinced it's true.

It's hard for first-chair Christians to survive and thrive in most churches.

Why? Because second-chair Christians dominate most churches. And they make it hard for first-chair Christians to stay in the first chair unless they keep their passion for God to themselves. But that's impossible for a first-chair Christian.

Dogs and Cats

Being a second-chair Christian is popular in America because it's comfortable. It doesn't require much. It keeps God at a comfortable distance, but close enough that He can come running when we need something.

It's similar to the picture I painted for you at the beginning of this chapter—when I treated Lisa like she was my servant. That's the way second-chair Christians treat God. They treat Him like He exists to serve them, rather than the other way around.

I once heard a preacher compare Christians to dogs and cats. He said when you pet a dog, it thinks, "Wow! *You* must be God!" But when you pet a cat, it thinks, "Wow! *I* must be God!"

Second-chair Christians are a lot more like cats than dogs. They treat God like He exists to serve them.

Not only that, their spiritual lives are cold, passionless, and fireless. The flame of their faith is barely lit. They're often apathetic, hypocritical, and complacent.

They don't have much of a relationship with God, so they don't act very Godly. Instead, they act worldly because they spend most of their time pursuing worldly things.

In fact, you often can't tell second-chair Christians apart from those who don't have any relationship with Christ. Studies show that those who call themselves Christians have sex before marriage, indulge in pornography, and get divorced at nearly the same rate as those who don't call themselves Christians.

Hypocrites

I travel and speak all over the world, which means I'm on airplanes a lot. Every time I get on a plane, I try to strike up a conversation and share the gospel with the person I'm sitting next to. I'm not a jerk about it, and I don't beat them over the head with a Bible. I just take an interest in their lives and let them talk about themselves. Eventually, God opens a door for me to share with them about how much He loves them.

If the person I'm sitting next to is not a Christian, I usually ask why. It's a great discussion starter because I'm prepared to give an answer for nearly any intellectual problem they may have with Christianity. I can help them overcome their barriers.

But many of them have a problem with Christianity that I have no answer for.

They'll say something like: "You know, I'd become a Christian if it weren't for all of the hypocrites."

What am I supposed to say to that? It doesn't make sense to me, either! How can a person claim to have a relationship with Christ but not act any different than those who don't know Him?

Unbelievers will come to a church service to check it out and see if there's anything real about Christianity. They'll see a few first-chair Christians and recognize that they genuinely love Jesus. They'll recognize that they're not perfect, but they're passionate and excited about God.

Then these unbelievers will watch second-chair Christians and begin to doubt whether there's really anything real about Christianity.

They'll think to themselves, "Wait a minute. I do business with that guy. He sure acts different here than he does the rest of the week." Or they'll think, "I go to school with that girl. I'm not any worse than she is. She's a hypocrite!"

As I've interacted with high-school and college students over the years, I find myself wondering if some of them have multiple person-

alities. Many act one way at church, another way at school, and yet another way at home. It's as if they're three separate people!

And for unbelievers, it's a huge turn off.

It must break God's heart when He watches unbelievers walk away. And it must make Him angry to watch the complacency, apathy, and hypocrisy of second-chair Christians.

I can see Jesus standing ready—with whips and cords in His hands—to go into our churches and turn over some tables because we've sold Him out with our hypocrisy. I can feel His anger.

Who's going to listen? Who's going to stand up and say, "Enough of the hypocrisy! We can't live like this anymore! We're turning people off to God!"

Lukewarm
In the book of Revelation, God spoke a lot to second-chair Christians. Several times, He gave warnings.

God gave one of the warnings to the church of Laodicea (Revelation 3:15-16). He said, "I know your deeds. I wish you were hot or cold."

Now, before I get to the warning, let me give you some context for this verse. There were two streams that flowed through the city of Laodicea. One was hot and the other was cold. The hot stream was useful for many things like bathing, cooking, and washing. (I understand the hot springs still exist today.) The cold stream was useful to the Laodiceans for drinking water and cooling off during the summer months.

When the two streams came together near the city, their waters mixed together and turned lukewarm. And no one in the city used this water for anything. It was basically useless to them.

God said to the Laodiceans: "I wish you were hot or cold. But, because you are lukewarm, I am going to spew you out of my mouth." Another Bible translation uses the word "vomit" instead of "spew."

23

Apparently, the complacency of second-chair Christians makes God sick.

Maybe it sickens God to think of all the people second-chair Christians could bring to heaven with them. Maybe it sickens Him to think of how hard they're making it for first-chair Christians to thrive and do His will. Maybe it sickens Him to think of how much eternal, Kingdom work they could be doing with the time, talent, and treasure He's given them to steward.

A Christian who has forgotten his first love isn't doing much for God that matters for eternity. As far as God's plans go, the second-chair Christian is useless.

First Love

God gave another warning in Revelation to second-chair Christians. This one was to the church in Ephesus. This warning seems to be aimed at people who've been in the church for a while.

Here's some background: Jesus had risen from the dead around 33 A.D., but this warning was written in the book of Revelation in about 95 A.D. That means that about sixty-two years of church history had passed before the warning was written. That was plenty of time for the church to lose its passion for Jesus.

Over time, their passion had faded and their love had grown cold.

In Revelation 2:2-4, God said something like this (my paraphrase) to the Ephesians:

> *I know your deeds, your hard work, and your perseverance. Good job! And I know how well you guys know the Bible. Way to go! But there's one thing I hold against you:*
>
> *You've lost your first love.*
>
> *Do you remember what it was like when I first saved you from your sinful life and restored you to an amazing relationship with me? Do you remember how excited you were about me? Do you remember*

how you used to talk about me with joy and love in your heart? Do you remember how you wanted to know more about me and grow in your relationship with me? Do you remember how your times of prayer and worship never seemed to be long enough? You wanted so much more.

Do you remember?

That's the kind of relationship I want with you. It's time to return to that kind of love again!

Is that what God is saying to you right now? He didn't just speak those words for the Ephesians. They're just as relevant for your life as they were two millennia ago.

If He's convicting your heart, then don't wait. Go back and reclaim that kind of relationship with Him. God hasn't moved away. You have.

I'm sure you've done a lot of good things for God. Maybe you've given to the poor or served your neighbors. Maybe you're an usher, youth sponsor, or children's worker at your church. Maybe you're a deacon or elder. Maybe you're even a pastor.

It doesn't matter. Whoever you are or whatever you do, you have to ask yourself if you've forsaken your first love. If you have, you're sitting in the second chair. Don't let anyone or anything stop you from repenting and getting back in the first chair.

Over time, passion fades and love grows cold.

It's time for you to return to your first love.

Chapter 3

THE THIRD CHAIR // Deceived

A NUMBER OF YEARS AGO, a pastor of a large church came down to the altar after I had given an invitation at an event where I was speaking. He was trembling and sobbing.

I put my hand on his shoulder and said, "How can I help you, brother?"

"I'm lost," he said in a shaky voice.

"Okay, let's get busy," I quickly replied. "How do you know you're lost?"

"I'm a pastor. I know what it means to be lost. And I'm lost!" he snapped back.

"Are you sure you don't just want to rededicate your life to Christ?"

He looked up at me, peered intensely into my eyes, and said with great resolve, "Don't you talk me out of getting saved!"

He then fell on his face and started weeping out loud, saying, "Lord, Jesus, I've been faking it all my life."

Sometimes, looks can be deceiving.

Lost

More recently, I was speaking at a conference for Christian athletes when a football player from Florida State University stood up, raised his tree-trunk arms in the air and said, "I've finally figured out what my problem is!"

He had our attention.

"All my life, I grew up in church," he continued. "I 'became a Christian' because it was important to my family. It was fun to be in church. I learned how to look good on the outside, while I was a mess on the inside. I did whatever I wanted when people weren't looking. I knew how to get away with anything. I knew how to be really sweet around my girlfriend's parents so they would think I was a good, Christian guy."

"Now, I know what my problem is," he repeated.

"I'm lost! I've never had a *real* relationship with Jesus!"

He fell down on the ground and cried out, "Oh Lord, Jesus. I give you my life. I'm so sorry."

Like I said, looks can be deceiving.

Insidious

The third chair is an insidious place to be. Do you know what the word *insidious* means? It means that something is dangerous, but you don't know it's dangerous.

Most people in the third chair have been taught things about God and the Bible. They might be interested in God, read about Him, and even ask questions about Him. But in the end, their intellectual knowledge doesn't lead them into a relationship with God.

Often, people in the third chair think they're saved. But they're not. They're deceived.

You might think there aren't a lot of people sitting in this chair. In reality, the third chair may be fuller than the first and second chairs combined.

Billy Graham once speculated that a significant percentage of those who attend churches across our nation are not Christians.

I once had a phone conversation with T.W. Hunt, a man who has a reputation for praying eight hours a day and who previously led the national prayer ministry for a large denomination. I asked him if it's possible that people could say they're a Christian and not be.

He paused for a moment and then began weeping.

"Adrian, I believe that at least eighty percent of the people on our denomination's rolls may not be Christians." He continued, "Oh Adrian, please do something about it!"

Of course, none of us really knows what percentage of people in the church is sitting in the third chair. But it's scary that some of our most respected church leaders estimate the percentage to be so high.

One reason it's so hard to know is because you can't always tell who's in the second chair and who's in the third. They act a lot alike.

The real difference is in their state of heart. And who fully knows that except God?

Jesus once said:
> "Not everyone who says to me, 'Lord, Lord,' will enter the kingdom of heaven, but only he who does the will of my Father who is in heaven. Many will say to me on that day, 'Lord, Lord, did we not prophesy in your name, and in your name drive out demons and perform many miracles?' Then I will tell them plainly, 'I never knew you. Away from me, you evildoers'" (Matthew 7:21-23).

Jesus made it clear that you can do a lot of good things that make you look like a Christian and still not make it into Heaven. You can even do powerful acts of ministry and still not make it into Heaven.

Looks can be deceiving…but not to God.

You can't fake your way into Heaven.

This Is a Test

Not sure if you're in the third chair? Test yourself. The Apostle Paul said: "...test the Spirit to see if you are in the faith. Do you not know that Christ is in you, unless of course, you fail the test?" (2 Corinthians 13:5).

There are at least three tests given in Scripture that can help you understand whether or not you're a true follower of Christ. The first test is whether or not you have an increasing measure of the "fruits of the spirit" in your life. What is this fruit? It's the inner qualities that should naturally flow into the actions of your life. Paul gave a list of these qualities in Galatians 5:22-23: love, joy, peace, patience, kindness, goodness, faithfulness, gentleness, and self-control.

Are you always arguing with your spouse or parents? Do you find that you have little self control with food, alcohol, pornography, and other things in your life? Do you lack peace or patience in your life? Are you consistently harsh in the ways you treat your family, friends, or co-workers? Are you absorbed in your own world and not serving others with kindness and goodness?

Those could be warning lights that you're sitting in the third chair.

Just because you go to church and talk about God does not make you His follower. If His Spirit lives in you, there will be other characteristics—or fruit—that will be evident to all. They will be evident in the things you say. They will be evident in the way you act. And they will be evident in how you treat other people.

A second similar test is to examine how much of your life resembles the life of Jesus. 1 John 2:6 says, "...those who claim to be Christians ought to walk as Jesus walked."

John also says in His first letter: "These things are written to those who believe that they would know for sure that they have eternal life." When John talks about "These things," he's referring to the whole content of the book of 1 John. It's one of the toughest books in Scripture, especially when it comes to obedience, love, and spiritual growth. It often holds up Jesus as our model and standard.

Those who follow Jesus look more and more like Him in the ways they live their lives.

The third test is God's conviction of sin in your life. Paul said in Ephesians 1:13-14 that when you're a Christian, you're sealed with the Holy Spirit. And Romans 1:16 says that the Spirit of God communicates with our spirit. So, when we sin, God's Spirit lets us know He's grieved. This is called conviction.

If you've been lying, stealing, cheating (on taxes, homework, or anything else), gossiping, or lusting—and it does not bother you—then you may be sitting in the third chair.

The Worst Verse
As I'm speaking in venues all over the country, I ask Christians if they know any Bible verses by heart. Most immediately start quoting John 3:16.

To me, John 3:16 is the worst verse in the Bible, and I'm not exaggerating. As a matter of fact, there are times when I can't stand that verse. It makes me mad! Not because I don't think it's true and life changing. But because I think it's the most misunderstood verse in the Bible.

Perhaps you memorized it when you were a kid: "For God so loved the world that he gave his one and only Son, that whoever **believes** in him will not perish but have eternal life" (John 3:16, emphasis added).

The reason we misunderstand this verse is because we don't understand what the word *believe* means. It doesn't mean to us what it meant when John wrote it two thousand years ago.

A lot of people *believe* that the Orthodox Christian understanding of Jesus is true. They *believe* Jesus is the Son of God; they *believe* He's one hundred percent God and one hundred percent man; they *believe* He died on a cross and rose from the dead three days later to provide forgiveness for sins.

But these are intellectual beliefs—the kind that can be disconnected from the rest of a person's life. They're an agreement that something is factual, similar to saying, "I believe Abraham Lincoln was once President of the United States."

You can intellectually believe that Honest Abe was one of our presidents without letting that fact have any real influence on your life. Without letting it affect your words and actions.

That's not the kind of belief that John was talking about in his gospel.

John 3:16 isn't just a verse. It's one sentence taken from a conversation between Jesus and a very religious man named Nicodemus. Nicodemus was a Pharisee, and he had likely memorized the entire Old Testament.

As Jesus talked to Nicodemus about the importance of *believing* (in verse 16), He also gave Nicodemus an Old Testament context (in verses 14-15) for what the word *believe* really meant.

Jesus said, "Just as Moses lifted up the snake in the desert, so the Son of Man is going to be lifted up so that everyone who **believes** will have everlasting life" (John 3:14-15, emphasis mine).

While this Old Testament reference to Moses and the Israelites (found in Numbers 21) is lost on most of us today, Nicodemus would have immediately understood what Jesus was referring to. Remember, he probably knew the Old Testament, word for word.

Snakes in the Desert
Numbers 21 tells us that the Israelites (roughly three and half million of them) were traveling toward the Red Sea. They had been in the desert for approximately thirty-eight years, and they were growing impatient. They were ready for better living conditions. They were ready to have a permanent home, in some place other than the desert. And they grumbled against God and Moses:

> "Why have you brought us up out of Egypt to die in the desert?" [they complained]. "There is no bread! There is no water! And we detest this miserable food!" (Numbers 21: 4-5).

The "miserable food" they detested was something called *manna*, which was like bread. God had faithfully provided them with manna every morning for thirty-eight years.

But the Israelites were tired of manna. Can you blame them? There probably wasn't a whole lot they could do to make manna taste good. I suppose they could make manna mush, manna pancakes, and manna waffles (without the syrup, of course). And if they got really creative, they could make mana-cotti (without the marinara sauce).

Get the picture? The Israelites weren't very thrilled about manna— or about running around in the desert, for that matter. They had decided that they wanted to go back to Egypt—back to slavery!

But God had something else in mind:

> "Then the Lord sent venomous snakes among them. They bit the Israelites, and many Israelites died" (Numbers 21:6).

I studied biology (and took lots of science classes) in college, and I've always liked snakes. I've studied them, and I love to handle them. I'll grab them by the back of the head and let them wrap around my arm. It's pretty cool.

The snake mentioned in Numbers 21:6 is probably a sand viper, a desert snake that's mentioned in other places in Scripture. Sand vipers are scary-looking snakes with eyeballs on top of their heads and two horns sticking up out of their eyes.

They look like little Satans.

And their venom is deadly. Once it enters a person's bloodstream, it causes the blood cells to become elongated so they won't fit into the capillaries of the hands and feet, ear lobes, and nose. This causes the extremities to swell, and eventually the capillaries rip open and fill the organs with blood. The organs then explode and a person bleeds to death.

And the whole process takes ten painful hours!

33

So, what does all this talk about snakes have to do with the word *believe* found in John 3? Hang on, we're just about there.

> *"[The Israelites] said, Moses, tell the Lord we're sorry. We sinned when we spoke against the Lord and against you. Pray that the Lord will take the snakes away from us"* (Numbers 21:7).

This was the first time in thirty-eight years that the Israelites had repented for any of their disbelief and disobedience. It was the first time they realized their sins were against God.

This is crucial to understanding the word *believe*.

Have you ever realized that your sins hurt God? Your lying, cheating, and stealing hurts Him! It's as though you've walked up to Jesus, slapped Him in the face, and told Him that His death for you means nothing.

> *"So Moses prayed for the people. The Lord said to Moses, 'Make a snake out of bronze, put it up on a pole. Then, when anyone is bitten, they can look at it and live.'*
>
> *"Moses made a snake out of bronze and put it up on a pole. Whenever someone was bitten by a snake, they looked at the pole and lived"* (Numbers 21:8-9).

That's what it means to truly *believe*.

Picture this: An Israelite is walking along—minding his own business—and a snake strikes him on the back of the leg. He has a choice to make. Does he really *believe* that looking at the bronze snake on Moses' pole will heal him?

It's really easy to know if he believes. How? Because if he really does, he will look at the pole. Duh! It's that simple.

So, let's make this personal. A snake bites you. You know you're going to die a slow, agonizing death over the next ten hours. What do you do? If you *believe*, you'll do whatever it takes to look at that bronze snake. You'll run as fast as you can to find it. You'll beg someone to

carry you if you can't walk on your own. You'll crawl if you have to!

That's what it means to *believe*. It means being convinced that something is true *and then aligning your life and your actions with that truth.*

That's what Jesus was telling Nicodemus when He said, "Just as Moses lifted up the snake in the desert, so the Son of Man is going to be lifted up so that everyone who believes will have everlasting life" (John 3:14-15).

The words *lifted up* in this reference—and every other reference in the book of John—meant "crucified on a cross." Do you remember when Jesus said, "If I be lifted up, I will draw all men unto me" (John 12:32)? He was referring to His crucifixion.

Jesus had to be *lifted up* (crucified) because every one of us is "snake-bitten" with sin. Without Jesus, we'd die because of our sin. And it would be a violent death!

But just as God made a way for people to be healed of their snake-bites when Moses *lifted up* the bronze snake, so He also made a way for us to be healed of our sin because Jesus was *lifted up* on a cross.

Salvation, then, is not just casually glancing at Jesus on the cross and saying you believe. It's desperately wanting Jesus more than you want air. It's racing toward His gracious cure for your sin just like you would race for the anecdote for a venomous snake bite.

That's what it means to really believe. *That's* what it means to really be saved.

If you haven't realized how much your sin hurts God, then you may be in the third chair. If you haven't turned to Jesus in desperation—knowing you can't find healing for your sin anywhere else—then you may be in the third chair. If your belief hasn't made a difference in how you live your life, then you may be in the third chair.

Looks can be deceiving. Don't be deceived.

Chapter 4

THE FOURTH CHAIR // Lost

A NUMBER OF YEARS AGO, when my son Branson was five years old, we were at a service where a speaker was giving an invitation for people to come to the altar and receive Christ. Midway through the invitation, Branson looked up at me and said, "Dad, I want to get saved."

I didn't think he knew what it meant to "get saved." I thought he was too young. Maybe he had heard me talk with someone else about "getting saved." Maybe he had heard me use those words, and he wanted to talk like his dad.

"We'll talk about it when we get home, son," I said to him, thinking he'd forget about it.

"Dad, I want to get saved right now!" he said with greater resolve.

He seemed sincere, but I was convinced no five-year-old kid could understand something as deep and profound as salvation.

"Okay, son," I replied. "When we get home."

He was quiet for a moment, and then he looked up at me with tears in his eyes.

"Dad, I have all these sins on my mind, and I want to get rid of them. I want to get saved, but you won't let me! Why not?"

I was shocked. I realized he knew exactly what he needed to do, and that night, my five-year-old son took a seat in the first chair. If you're in the fourth chair, so can you.

It's time for you to get into the first chair.

The Lifejacket

If you're in the fourth chair, you're spiritually lost. That's not a slam on you, it's just a reality that you must face up to. Maybe you've never been told the Good News about Jesus and His forgiveness for your sins, or maybe you've heard about it but never personally accepted it.

Either way, you're wandering on a road that will lead you to destruction—in this life and in eternity. The Good News is that there's a different road. But you have to recognize your need for it.

That's what Branson recognized, even at his young age. He knew that he'd sinned, and he knew that his sins had hurt God. He knew that only God could wipe away the guilt and shame he was feeling. That's why I believed he was ready to ask God for forgiveness that night.

Likewise, if you're sitting in the fourth chair, you don't have to stay there. But you have to understand that you've sinned against God, and only He can forgive you and bring new life to your dead spirit.

You're spiritually drowning, and you need a life jacket.

A man who doesn't know he's drowning probably won't cry out for a lifejacket. But a man who knows he's drowning is desperate. He's not going to politely whisper, "Excuse me. Could someone please pass me a lifejacket?"

He's going to scream out for the one thing he knows will save him: "Help! I need a lifejacket!"

You must understand your need for God. You need Him desperately. He's the only one who can forgive you of your sins and save you from spiritual death and eternal destruction in Hell.

He'll hand-deliver you a lifejacket…if you'll call on Him.

It's time for you to get into the first chair.

Hypocrites
Now, if you're in the fourth chair and you're reading this book, it's because you're brilliant. Only a brilliant, fourth-chair person could get this far. You're checking things out. Perhaps the Spirit of God is drawing you.

You know people in the first chair. They stand out. You also know of the masses that are in the second and third chairs. They turn you off.

Time out: I want to apologize right now for those of us who've been in the second chair. I've found myself often sliding into it, and I'm sorry that I've turned you off. No excuses!

But as brilliant as you are, you're not being very smart at this moment. You're letting people in the second chair (the "puke chair," as I call it) be closer to God than you are.

I meet fourth-chair people all the time who say they aren't going to become a Christian because of all the (second-chair) hypocrites they see in the church.

That reasoning seems pretty flawed to me. It seems more like an excuse.

It's like saying that you're not going to grab a lifejacket yourself because you don't like the way some people act after they've put on their lifejacket. I agree—they act like they're still drowning. I don't like it either!

But I'm not going to let that keep *me* from being rescued from drowning.

39

If *you* don't grab the lifejacket, *you* are going to drown—regardless of what other people are doing. It's as simple as that.

When *you* die and face God's Judgment, He's not going to hold *you* accountable for what others did with the lifejackets He threw them. He's going to hold *you* accountable for what *you* did with the lifejacket He threw *you*.

Are you going to grab it and let Him save you, or are you going to keep flailing on your own until you finally drown?

If you let God save you, then you can call out the hypocrites in the second chair to live as a preview of heaven, not hell. You can call them to act like their saved instead of acting like they're still drowning. And, who knows, God may end up using you to throw a lifejacket to others in the third chair.

You know what I call that? Revival! I've noticed that when fourth-chair people get right with God, they often start revivals around them. Why? Because people who've been forgiven much, love much (Luke 7:47).

This is the most important decision you'll ever make. Don't let anything stop you from grabbing the lifejacket before this day ends. Don't wait! God is moving in your heart now.

It's time for you to get into the first chair.

Chapter 5

TRADING PLACES

SO, WHICH CHAIR ARE YOU SITTING IN?

If you're sitting in the first chair, I want to encourage you to never give up your seat there. Don't let people sitting in other chairs make you feel abnormal. In God's eyes, you're living out what He wants for all of our lives. That makes you the normal one—even though you stand out in this world.

Remember, it's easy to grow cold over time. Guard your heart.

If you're in the second, third, or fourth chairs, it's time for you to make a decision.

If you're not sure which of two chairs you're in, it usually means that you're in the higher-numbered one. This is especially important to understand if you're trying to figure out if you're in the second or third chair.

It doesn't really matter, though. Either way, God is calling you to move to the first chair.

It's your choice. You can stay where you are, or you can answer God's call by making the move. If you do, it will be the greatest decision you've ever made. You'll know the full joy of God's forgiveness. You'll understand your true purpose in life. (You'll be passionately living for the only cause that's really worth living for!) You'll know how incredible it is to have a deep, intimate relationship with God that overflows into the rest of your life. And you'll live with God forever in Heaven.

But the choice comes with a cost. It requires that you humbly bow your heart before Jesus, recognizing your desperate need for Him. It requires that you confess your sins to Him and truly believe in Him *with your whole life*. It requires that you surrender your life to God's ways and purposes and place your full trust in Him to provide for every spiritual, physical, and emotional need you have. That's what it means to live in the first chair.

So, I'm giving you an invitation today—just like I give audiences at events where I speak. The invitation is for you to place your full *trust* in God. In the Old Testament, the word translated as *trust* is the Hebrew word *batach*. It literally means to lie flat on your face.

That's what I'm asking you to do. As you place your trust in God with your heart and mouth, I'm asking you to find a place where you can also trust Him with your whole being by lying flat on your face before Him. That's true *batach*.

You might be saying to yourself, "Who does he think I am? Some kind of wacko? Some kind of freak?"

No, I don't think you're a wacko, but your commitment to Jesus should be so complete that you're willing to look like one for His sake. That's what it means to sit in the first chair. You're totally His. And you don't care what anyone else thinks. That's why I'm asking you to humbly get on your face before Him now.

Unashamed
When I was in seminary, I attended a lot of chapel services. But one stands out more than most. A guy wearing a really nice suit was preaching his heart out—and it was a good message. But there was nothing really unique about it until he got down on his hands and knees and pretended that he was kissing the ground and groveling

before God. He said he was willing to humble himself that much before God—and he didn't care what anyone else thought.

Everything inside of me wanted to scream out to him, "Would you get off the ground? You're embarrassing yourself! You're embarrassing me!"

Time out: Let me help you understand where I was coming from.

I was raised in a tough family. My dad taught me that men don't cry. And they sure don't get down on their knees and grovel before anyone. He told my three brothers and me that we could never start a fight, but if someone else started one, it was our job to finish it.

And we finished a lot of fights—until people started realizing that if they fought one of us, they'd have to fight all of us.

That's the environment I was raised in.

So, when I saw that preacher groveling on his hands and knees, I was embarrassed and even disgusted. Then God spoke to me. He didn't speak in an audible voice. It was actually louder than that. He spoke to me in my spirit.

"Adrian, are you ashamed of me?" He asked. I was startled at how clear I "heard" Him.

"Would you get on your face before me right now—in front of all these people," He continued, "or do you care more about what these people think than what I think?"

I responded to God at that very moment. I said, "God, I don't care what anybody else on this planet thinks about me. I'm seeking after your praise and not the praise of men.

"I will get on my face before you—anytime and anyplace!"

After that experience, I began to notice how many people in the Gospels fell on their face before Jesus. Even a guy controlled by evil spirits ran up to Jesus and fell on his face before Him. (Even a bunch of demons humbled themselves before God!)

We're never told in Scripture to fall on our face, but everybody knew in those days that that's what the Hebrew word for *trust* meant. So, when they put their trust in God, they fell on their face before Him.

And that's my invitation to you—that you would literally fall on your face before God as you place your trust in Him with your heart, mouth, and your whole being.

I Surrender All

Clay Crosse's song "I Surrender All" changed my life. I was speaking at a youth camp where they were acting out a mime to this song. As the song played, several kids used rope to tie another kid to a cross. For the last half of the song, the kid hung from the cross—completely silent and still.

It demanded a response. Even though I was the speaker, I went forward and lied down in front of the kid, symbolizing my trust in Jesus.

In that moment I said to Jesus, "Everything I have is yours. I don't care what anybody else thinks about me because I know that you gave everything for me."

I got in the first chair at that moment, and I've tried not to give up my place there since. I haven't trusted in my own strength to stay there, but rather the strength that God has given me. It's been a battle at times, but it's one worth fighting.

As you place your full trust in Him, I leave you with the words to "I Surrender All"—the song God used to change my life. Feel free to sing or pray these words to God as the cry of your heart.

I Surrender All
Lyrics by Clay Crosse

I have wrestled in the darkness of this lonely pilgrim land
Raising strong and mighty fortresses that I alone command
But these castles I've constructed by the strength of my own hand
Are just temporary kingdoms on foundations made of sand
In the middle of the battle I believe I've finally found
I'll never know the thrill of victory 'til I'm willing to lay down
All my weapons of defense and earthly strategies of war
So I'm laying down my arms and running helplessly to Yours

I surrender all my silent hopes and dreams
Though the price to follow costs me everything
I surrender all my human soul desires
If sacrifice requires
That all my kingdoms fall
I surrender all

If the source of my ambition is the treasure I obtain
If I measure my successes on a scale of earthly gain
If the focus of my vision is the status I attain
My accomplishments are worthless and my efforts are in vain

So I lay aside these trophies to pursue a higher crown
And should You choose somehow to use the life I willingly lay down
I surrender all the triumph for it's only by Your grace
I relinquish all the glory, I surrender all the praise

Everything I am, all I've done, and all I've known
Now belongs to You, the life I live is not my own
Just as Abraham laid Isaac on the sacrificial fire
If all I have is all that You desire
I surrender all

A Final Prayer

Lord, I pray in Jesus' name, that you'll help readers of this book to consider where they sit with you. And I pray that you'll help them say these words and live them out through their life: "I don't care what anyone else thinks about me, I place my full trust in you. And I surrender everything to you. With Your help, I want to stay in the first chair for the rest of my life. In Jesus' name, amen."

Lord, let no one be kept from surrendering all.

Let no one be kept from sitting in the first chair.

> If the content of this book has impacted your life in any way, we'd love to hear about it. Please email us at laborers@kbm.org.

CHECK OUT THESE ADDITIONAL RESOURCES BY ADRIAN DESPRES AND KBM MEDIA

The Four Chairs
(CD or DVD)
If you liked the book, check out Adrian's live presentation of *The Four Chairs* message in audio or video formats. The video is great for use as an evangelistic tool in small-group settings.

(front)

(back)

The Four Chairs
T-shirt
Wear The Four Chairs message on a T-shirt and be ready to answer when friends ask you what it means. It's a great evangelism tool.
Colors: Grey, Pink, Black.
Sizes: YL, S-XXL

Bricks & Sticks
(DVD)
We each build our lives with some kind of building material. Some materials last. Some don't. In this message, Adrian asks you to examine what kinds of material you are using to build your life? Will it last for eternity?

MORE BY ADRIAN DESPRES AND KBM MEDIA

The Worst Verse
(CD)
For Adrian, John 3:16 is the worst verse in the Bible. Yes, it has the potential to be a powerful, life-changing verse. The problem is, it's one of the most misunderstood verses in the Bible. Join Adrian on a journey back into the Old Testament to see what John 3:16 really means, and why it could ultimately be the best verse in your life.

Delighted in Suffering
(CD)
Most of us avoid suffering. We despise it. But not the Apostle Paul—he delighted in suffering! In this message, Adrian helps you understand what the Bible has to say about suffering and how you can delight in it—even as Paul did.

You can purchase each of these resources by logging onto www.kbm.org or by calling 1-800-873-8957.

www.kbm.org
www.adriandespres.org